Rough Guides

25 Ultimate experiences

South America

Make the most of your time on Earth

ROUGH
GUIDES

25 YEARS 1982–2007

NEW YORK • LONDON • DELHI

Contents

3

Introduction

EXPERIENCES have always been at the heart of the Rough Guide concept. A group of us began writing the books **25 years ago** (hence this celebratory mini series) and wanted to share the kind of travels we had been doing ourselves. It seems bizarre to recall that in the early 1980s, travel was very much a minority pursuit. Sure, there was a lot of tourism around, and that was reflected in the guidebooks in print, which traipsed around the established sights with scarcely a backward look at the local population and their life. We wanted to change all that: to put a country or a city's popular culture centre stage, to highlight the clubs where you could hear local music, drink with people you hadn't come on holiday with, watch the local football, join in with the festivals. And of course we wanted to push travel a bit further, inspire readers with the confidence and knowledge to break away from established routes, to find pleasure and excitement in remote islands, or desert routes, or mountain treks, or in street culture.

Twenty-five years on, that thinking seems pretty obvious: we all want to experience something real about a destination, and to seek out travel's **ultimate experiences**. Which is exactly where these **25 books** come in. They are not in any sense a new series of guidebooks. We're happy with the series that we already have in print. Instead, the **25s** are a collection of ideas, enthusiasms and inspirations: a selection of the very best things to see or do – and not just before you die, but now. Each selection is gold dust. That's the brief to our writers: there is no room here for the average, no space fillers. Pick any one of our selections and you will enrich your travelling life.

But first of all, take the time to browse. Grab a half dozen of these books and let the ideas percolate … and then begin making your plans.

Mark Ellingham
Founder & Series Editor, Rough Guides

25

Ultimate
experiences
South
America

Show no restraint at Carnaval in

01 Rio

Brazil has a monopoly on exhibitionism. There's no other country on the planet where the unbridled pursuit of pleasure is such a national obsession, transcending race, class and religion. Brazilian bacchanal reaches its apogee during Carnaval when the entire country enters into a collective state of alcohol-fuelled frenzy. Rio is the most glitzy and outrageous celebration of them all, an X-rated theatre of the absurd and the greatest spectacle of flesh, fetish and fantasy you are ever likely to see. For this four-day blowout before Lent the streets of the *Cidade Maravilhosa* are overrun with Amazonian-sized plumed headdresses, 100ft floppy carrots, cavorting frogs, drag queens and head-to-toe gilded supermodels clad in impossibly tiny tassels, sequins and strategically applied body paint, challenging the ban on complete nudity.

The centrepiece of Carnaval is the parade of the sixteen samba schools (a neighborhood association, there's nothing academic about it) along the half-mile parade strip of the colossal Sambódromo (a specially constructed parade stadium). Samba schools often hail from the poorest communities and spend nearly the entire year preparing a flamboyant allegory of their chosen theme which is dramatized through a highly choreographed display of impassioned song, wild dance, gigantic *papier mâché* figures, lavish costume and pulsating percussion.

It doesn't take long for such organized celebrations to erupt with infectious delirium as the whole city voraciously indulges in sensual pleasure at every turn – Rio's denizens, also known as *cariocas*, have never been known for their temperance. The neighborhood *blocos*, or parades, are the most accessible and impromptu way to immerse yourself in this sexually-charged atmosphere. In a free-wheeling, fantasy land where truly anything goes, even the most rigid of hips will gyrate freely and as the night unravels, the more you'll have to try to forget in the *manhã*.

need to know

Carnaval takes place from the Friday before Ash Wednesday. Tickets for the Sambódromo can cost anywhere from US$200 in the bleachers to more than US$1000 for a covered box, complete with celebrities and champagne. The rawness of Carnaval has been diluted by commercialism and the stage-managed protocol of the Sambódromo. For a more authentic experience, tag along with any of the local neighbourhood *blocos* – street parties in the truer sense, with trucks converted to moving stage sets, with bands, loud speakers, free-flowing *cachaça* and chaotic revelry.

02

Natural rejection in the GALÁPAGOS ISLANDS

" as you walk through this scarred landscape, you find that life abounds, albeit peculiar life **"**

The utter indifference, some call it fearlessness, that most of the animals of the Galápagos Islands show humans is as if they knew all along they'd be the ones to change humanity's perception of itself forever. It was, after all, this famous menagerie of accidental inmates washed or blown from the mainland across a thousand kilometres of ocean and cut off from the rest of their kind, that started the cogs turning in Charles Darwin's mind. His theory of natural selection changed humankind's understanding of its place in the world, and by extension some might say, its place in the universe.

Peering out to shore from your cabin, you little suspect that the neon sea and coral beaches mark not the fringes of paradise, but of hell solidified – a ferocious wasteland of petrified lava lakes, ash-striped cliffs, serrated clinker tracts and smouldering volcanoes. Even so, as you walk through this scarred landscape, you find that life abounds, albeit peculiar life, the product of many generations of adaptation to a comfortless home. A marine iguana flashes an impish grin at you and, unlike its more familiar ancestors on the continent, scuttles into the sea to feed. On a rocky spur nearby, another one-of-a-kind, a flightless cormorant, which long ago abandoned its aerial talents for ones nautical, hangs its useless wing-stumps out to dry. With each island, new animal oddities reveal themselves to you – giant tortoises, canoodling waved albatrosses, lumbering land iguanas, Darwin's finches to name but a few – each a key player in the world's most celebrated workshop of evolution. And except for the friendly mockingbirds that pick at your shoelaces, most life on Galápagos is blank to your existence, making you feel like a most privileged kind of gatecrasher, one who's allowed an up-close look at a long-kept secret: the mechanics of life on Earth.

need to know

An eight-day cruise is the best way to get a good overview of the islands, costing anything from US$60 per day for a last-minute deal on a small economy boat in low season (usually Feb to mid-June & Sept–Oct) to over US$400 a day on a luxury cruiser. Flights to the islands leave from Quito or Guayaquil in Ecuador; visitors have to pay a US$100 national park entrance fee on arrival.

Recently named the eighth "Great Wine Capital", putting it alongside more famous regions like Napa and Bordeaux, Mendoza is the main reason Argentina has become one of the top wine-producing countries in the world. The area attracts topflight vintners from around the world, though arguably the best wines in the region are those of Argentine Nicolás Catena. Even if you've already had the bacchanalian pleasure of uncorking one of his US$100 bottles, nothing can match the excitement of visiting his otherworldly winery, Bodega Catena Zapata, where the grapes are harvested from February to April.

Rising like a Mayan pyramid from the dusty flatlands that surround Mendoza, the adobe and glass structure stands against the breathtaking backdrop of the 6965m Aconcagua, the highest peak in the Americas. Descend through a pathway of stone arches into the building's cool, dimly lit sarcophagus, where the wine barrels are stored, and a long oak table is set with a sampler to quicken your pulse. It's the perfect setting for a taste of Mendoza's signature red grape, malbec, which has prospered like no other in this dry, high desert terroir. For decades after being brought over from Europe by Italian immigrants like Catena's grandfather, the ruby-colored grape was deemed too robust for all but the unfussy Argentine palate accustomed to a beef-heavy diet. Now widening curiosity among wine consumers and more consistent growing techniques have made this fruity and full-bodied nectar the latest toast of the wine world.

With hundreds of tasting rooms within reach – many in the traditional bodegas are still free – there's no shortage of places to visit. So get an early start, and unless you want to topple over in a sun-kissed, drunken haze, abide by the sommelier's golden rule: swirl 'n spit.

need to know

For more information on touring **Bodega Catena Zapata** in Luján de Cuyo, visit their website (ⓦwww.catenawines. com). There are also plenty of other bodegas to choose from. To tour the wineries on your own, pick up a road map from the tourist office and stores downtown; the best is produced by **Winemap** (ⓦwww.winemapargentina.com). You can also arrange tailor-made visits to the bodegas with specialists such as **Robertson Wine Tours** (ⓦwww.robertsonwinetours.com) or **Amazing Mendoza** (ⓦwww.amazingmendoza.com).

03 WINE TASTING
in Mendoza

TAPATI:
fun and games on
Easter
Island

04

Rapa Nui – Easter Island – is shrouded in mystery. How did its people get there? Where did they come from? How did they move those gigantic statues? Some of that enigma comes to life during the fortnight-long Tapati, a festival that combines ancient customs, such as carving and canoeing, with modern sports, like the triathlon and horseracing.

First, the islanders form two competing teams, representing the age-old clans, so if you want to participate, it's best to get to know one of the captains. The opening ceremony kicks off with Umu Tahu, a massive barbecue, followed by a parade of would-be carnival queens wearing traditional grass skirts.

Most of the sports events are for men only: one breathtaking highlight is the bareback horserace along Vaihu Beach. If you fancy your chances against the proud locals, be prepared to wear little more than a bandana, a skimpy sarong and copious body paint. Another event, staged in the majestic crater at Rano Raraku, has contestants – including the odd tourist – paddling across the lake in reed canoes, running round the muddy banks carrying two hands of bananas, and finally swimming across, with huge crowds cheering them on.

Meanwhile the womenfolk compete to weave the best basket, craft the most elegant shell necklace or produce the finest grass skirt; visitors are welcome to participate. Little girls and venerable matriarchs alike play leading roles in the after-dark singing and dancing contests. They croon and sway through the night, until the judges declare the winning team, usually around daybreak.

But the true climax is Haka Pei: three-dozen foolhardy athletes slide down the steep slopes of Maunga Pu'i Hill – lying on banana trunks. Top speeds reach 80kph, total chaos reigns and usually a limb or two is broken, but the crowds love it. Should they ask you to take part, learn two vital Rapa Nui words: *mauru uru*, no thanks.

need to know

Tapati begins every year at the end of January. Book your accommodation and LAN flight months ahead and get to the airport at least three hours before departure – overbooking is notorious. For more information, consult the Chilean tourist board site: ⊛www.sernatur.cl.

05

Driving across the

Salar de Uyuni

Driving across the immaculate white expanse of the Salar de Uyuni, with volcanic peaks lining the far horizon, you'd think you were on another planet, so alien and inhospitable is the terrain. Set at 3650m above sea level in the remote Andes of southwest Bolivia, the Salar is the largest salt flat in the world, a brilliant white and perfectly flat desert that stretches over 10,000 square km.

In some places the salt is over 120m deep, saturated with water but with a thick surface crust patterned with strange polygonal lines of raised salt crystals that add to the unearthly feel. When dry, the salt shines with such intensity you'll find yourself reaching down to check that it's not ice or snow. After a heavy rainfall, the Salar transforms into an immense mirror, reflecting the sky and the surrounding snow-capped peaks so pristinely that at times the horizon disappears and the mountains seem like islands floating in the sky. The best views are from Isla del Pescado, a rocky island at the centre of the Salar that's home to an extraordinary array of giant cactuses that somehow manage to thrive in this harsh saline environment.

To really appreciate the sheer scale and surreal beauty of the landscape, it's worth taking the full four-day tour, travelling right across the Salar in a 4WD and sleeping in rudimentary huts and shelters on the shores of the lake; you can even stay in a hotel made entirely from salt. These trips also take in the Eduardo Abaroa Andean Fauna National Reserve, south of the Salar, a windswept region of high altitude deserts, icebound volcanoes and mineral-stained lakes where you can see an unlikely variety of wildlife, including flocks of flamingos and herds of vicuña, the delicate and extremely rare wild relative of the llama.

need to know

Expeditions to visit the Salar by 4WD are easily arranged with local tour operators in the nearby town of Uyuni, a bleak, windswept railway town saved from oblivion by the arrival of tourism. Uyuni can be reached by road and rail from La Paz, which is an arduous twelve hours away. You can also get there on a once-weekly train across the border from Calama in northern Chile.

"So few people visit in fact that in 1976 the discovery of the pig-like Chaco peccary or tagua shook the zoological world – until then it was known only from fossils."

The faces in our safari party each wear the same expression of awe as we stare at the jaguar lazily strolling down the dusty track. This one looks a lot bigger than its TV counterparts and we feel a healthy sense of respect now that there's nothing but a clear path separating it from us. With paws the size of dinner-plates and a head as big as a sack of potatoes there is no doubt that he rules here, and we are tolerated by him just as we tolerate the gnats that buzz around our ears.

The scene plays out not in the lush, virgin Amazonia, or in the verdant, marshy Pantanal, but in the Paraguayan Chaco – one of the hottest, driest and most inhospitable environments on Earth. In spite of its image as a thorny, dusty wilderness, the unspoilt splendour of the High Chaco makes it one of the best places in South America for wildlife watching. Here big mammals still roam about in large numbers and encounter so few humans that they know no fear toward us. So few people visit in fact that in 1976 the discovery of the pig-like Chaco peccary or tagua shook the zoological world – until then it was known only from fossils.

From November through March the Chaco defies its popular arid image as heavy rains stimulate plant growth, converting dry grasslands to lush wetlands – a haven for waterbirds such as the enormous jabiru and flocks of snow-white egrets. Caiman sun themselves on sandbanks and herds of capybara take advantage of the season of plenty to raise their young.

As we watch, the jaguar moves off into the distance. Our driver restarts the engine to approach him. The jaguar turns abruptly, flashes us a look of contempt and disappears into the bush.

need to know

Getting into the High Chaco is difficult and not to be attempted alone – trips must be well planned and fully provisioned. Professional, expert-guided eco-tours are available through **FAUNA Paraguay** with prices depending on group size (inquire at Ⓔfaunaparaguay@ yahoo.com.ar). Public transport will take you only as far as the Mennonite colonies of Filadelfia and Loma Plata; there is no onward transport to the wilder areas from there.

A shard of sunlight cracks open the horizon, spilling crimson into the sky and across the last icy crest, glittering like a crown of diamonds above you. Your exhausted legs can barely lift your snow-encrusted boots and the crampons that stubbornly grip the ice, but you're almost at the top. Gasping in the thin air, you haul yourself from the chilly shadow of night into the daylight. As the sun bursts across your face, the most spectacular dawn you've ever seen spreads out before you.

The perfect cone of Volcán Cotopaxi, regarded by the early explorer Alexander von Humboldt as "the most beautiful and regular of all the colossal peaks in the high Andes", at 5897m is one of the highest and most magnificent active volcanoes in the world. From the refuge at 4800m, tucked just below a girdle of ice and snow encircling the peak, it's around six to eight gruelling hours to the summit, on a route that picks its way between gaping crevasses and fragile seracs, over ladders and up vertical ice. For some it's just as well that much of this steep climb is done unseen at night; hopefuls must rouse themselves from a fitful and breathless slumber at midnight to climb before the heat of the day makes the glacier unstable. The payback is arriving at the summit just as the sun rises, when you're treated to mind-blowing views of Cotopaxi's yawning crater, the giant peaks of the Andes in the distance, and through the clouds, glimpses of Quito sleeping far below.

07

Seeing the sun rise from
Volcán Cotopaxi

need to know The volcano is the centrepiece of the **Parque Nacional Cotopaxi** (daily 8am–5pm, last entrance 3pm; US$10), accessed from the Panamericana 41km south of Quito. Aspiring mountaineers need the services of a fully qualified guide available through the specialist climbing operators in Quito or Riobamba, who can also provide mountaineering equipment, instruction on how to use it and a programme for acclimatization.

08

Braving the wind in

Torres del Paine

You have to keep your head down. Despite the spray-laden wind, it's tempting to lift it above the rim of the boat and look ahead, so you can see the foam-capped waves racing past as the Zodiac inflatable roars upstream. Soon, in the distance, a towering peak of rock rises up. As you get closer you see shattering precipices and giant towers dusted with snow.

This is Torres del Paine, the citadel in Chile's epic south and one of the wildest national parks in the world. When the inboard of the Zodiac inflatable is finally switched off, all you can hear is the fury of the wind. The waves die down and the water reflects the massif in a pool as perfect as you could imagine, fringed by gnarled trees and blasted by bitter winds. Close by is a huge glacier, an offshoot of one of the largest ice fields in the world.

Then you set off walking, shifting the weight of your pack to get comfortable. There are other hikers around you too – this isn't deserted wilderness by any means – but the largeness of the landscape can more than accommodate everyone. High up to the east, and overlooking the scrub and blasted forest, are the unnaturally sculpted Paine Towers themselves, and in front of you, dark-capped, are weird sculptures of the peaks of the Cuernos del Paine. If you're lucky you'll stumble across some guanacos, wild relations of the llama, or even a shy ñandú, the South American ostrich. But perhaps the best experience to be had here is simply to inhale the air, which is so crisp and thin that breathing is like drinking iced water.

need to know

There are two main trails: the Circuit, which is a six- to seven-day walk around the whole massif, and the "W" (because that's what it looks like on a map), which takes four to five days. Be prepared for wind, wet and cold. Guided treks run from nearby Puerto Natales, or travel to the park on your own by bus or Zodiac inflatable. Park admission is CH$10,000 (about US$20).

23

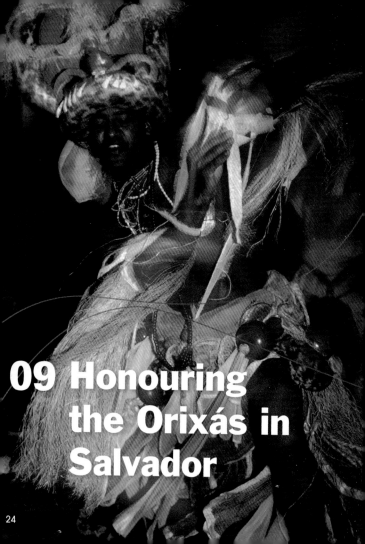

09 Honouring the Orixás in Salvador

You don't have to look far to have an out-of-body experience in Salvador. Along the "Red Beach" of Salvador da Bahia, worshippers dressed in ethereal white robes gather around sand-altars festooned with gardenias. Some may fall into trances, writhing on the beach, screaming so intensely you'd think they were being torn limb from limb. Perhaps in more familiar settings you'd be calling an ambulance, but this is Salvador, the epicentre of the syncretic African-based religion known as candomblé, in which worshippers take part in *toques*, a ritual that involves becoming possessed by the spirit of their Orixá.

A composite of Portuguese Catholicism and African paganism, candomblé is most fervently practiced in Salvador, but it defines the piquancy and raw sensuality of Brazilian soul throughout the entire country. In this pagan religion, each person has an Orixá or protector god from birth who personifies a natural force, such as fire or water, and is allied to an animal, colour, day of the week, food, music and dance. The ceremonies are performed on sacred ground called *terreiros* and typically feature animal sacrifices, hypnotic drumming, chanting and convulsing. Props and paraphernalia are themed accordingly; the house is decorated with the color of the honorary Orixá, and usually the god's favourite African dish is served.

Ceremonies are specialized for each god, but no matter which Orixá you are celebrating, you can be sure that the experience

❝ Some may fall into trances, writhing on the beach, screaming so intensely you'd think they were being torn limb from limb. ❞

will rank among the most bizarre of your life. If you attend a ritual for Ossaim, the Orixá of leaves, for example, chances are that you will be swept from head to foot in foliage. If pyrotechnics is your thing, better pay homage to Xango, god of fire, whose ceremony reaches a rather hazardous climax as bowls of fire are passed, head to head, among the participants. While animal sacrifice, one central aspect of the ceremony, may not be for the faint-hearted, music and feasting provide a more universally palatable denouement to the public "mass". After you enter the realm of candomblé, you may view Salavador and indeed Brazil through an ethereal prism that challenges your excepted reason.

need to know

There are frequent, direct flights to Salvador from Rio. The airport is 20km north of the centre. Visitors are admitted to *terreiros* (sacred ceremonial sites) and "mass" usually begins in the early evening and continues until midnight. Trousers and long skirts should be worn, preferably white. For further information on when and where ceremonies are held in Salvador, contact the **Federação Baiana de Culto Afro-Brasileiro** (Rua Portas do Carmo, 39; ☎3326-6969).

10
CELEBRATE *Qoyllur Riti*

Most visitors to the ancient Inca capital of Cusco in southern Peru are drawn by the extraordinary ruined temples and palaces and the dramatic scenery of the high Andes. But the only way to get to the heart of the indigenous Andean culture is to join a traditional fiesta. Nearly every town and village in the region engages in these raucous and chaotic celebrations, a window on a secret world that has survived centuries of oppression.

Of all the fiestas, the most extraordinary and spectacular is Qoyllur Riti, held at an extremely high altitude in a remote Andean valley to the south of Cusco. Here, you can join tens of thousands of indigenous pilgrims as they trek up to a campsite at the foot of a glacier to celebrate the reappearance of the Pleiades constellation in the southern sky – a phenomenon that has long been used to predict when crops should be planted. At the heart of the fiesta are young men dressed in ritual costumes of the Ukuku, a half-man, half-bear trickster hero from Andean mythology, and if you're hardy enough, you can join them as they climb even higher to spend the night singing, dancing and engaging in ritual combat on the glacier itself. Be warned, though, that this is an extreme celebration. When the pilgrim-celebrants descend from the mountain at first light, waving flags and toting blocks of ice on their backs, they also carry the bodies of those who've died during the night, frozen or fallen into crevasses, their blood sacrifice at once mourned and celebrated as vital to the success of the agricultural year ahead.

need to know

Qoyllur Riti happens in early May just before Corpus Christi – you can arrange transport to the start of the trek near the town of Ocongate with tour companies in Cusco itself. However, year-round there's almost always a fiesta going on somewhere in the region, and the best are often those you stumble across by accident. A comprehensive list of Cusco's fiestas can be found at Ⓦwww.cuscoperu.com.

You can bet that the great riches that flowed through Cartagena during colonial times proved an irresistible attraction to the pirates and privateers that roamed the Caribbean. Founded nearly five centuries ago as Cartagena de Indias – the Carthage of the Indies – this was one of the most strategically vital points in the Spanish empire. It was here that the galleon fleets would gather before making the perilous return journey to Spain, their holds laden with the gold and silver looted from the great indigenous civilizations of the Americas. Here, too, was the empire's main slave market, a clearing-house for the ill-fated Africans whose blood and sweat underwrote the entire colonial venture.

Though the Spanish have long since departed, Cartagena's colonial heritage is inescapable. The narrow, winding streets of the old walled city are still lined with grand mansions painted in the vibrant pastel hues of the Caribbean, with overhanging balconies draped in flowers and arched doorways that lead into cool courtyard gardens. Its nightclubs and rum shops pulsate with salsa, cumbia and reggaeton – African rhythms little changed from those brought over in the first slave ships. As you wander down these almost fantastical, decaying streets, it's easy to understand how this city inspired Colombia's greatest author, Gabriel García Márquez, to create his masterpieces of magical realism.

Stop for a coffee in the run-down artisans' neighbourhood of Getsemaní, or cool off with a freshly blended tropical fruit juice by the docks, and you could be rubbing shoulders with Marxist guerillas plotting against the government, cocaine traffickers planning their next shipment, emerald smugglers cutting a deal, or just a local hustler cooking up his latest scam. In the country of dreams as the locals call it – anything is possible.

need to know

Cartagena is around 650km north of the Colombian capital, Bogotá, approximately 24 hours by bus, though military roadblocks and Colombia's precarious security situation can cause lengthy delays. It's much easier to take a local flight, which is reasonably priced and takes only 2.5–3 hours.

11 Navigating the
NARROW STREETS
of *Cartagena*

Just about every traveller is struck at some point with the panic-inducing realization that there are people back home expecting to be lavished with exotic gifts from faraway lands. If you happen to find yourself in Ecuador at this anxiety-ridden moment you're in luck: Otavalo's spectacular indigenous artesanías market is one of the largest crafts fairs on the continent and one of the most enjoyable alfresco retail experiences to be had anywhere.

Up for grabs are handicrafts of every description – ceramics, jewellery, paintings, musical instruments, carvings and above all a dazzling array of weavings and textiles for which the Otavalo Valley has long been famous. Looms in back rooms across the countryside clatter away to produce chunky sweaters, hats, gloves, trousers and tablecloths, while weavings of the highest quality, indigenous ponchos, blouses, belts and tapestries are still made by master-craftsmen using traditional means in tiny village workshops. Come Saturday, when the crafts market combines with a general produce, hardware and animal market to create a megabazaar that engulfs much of the town, people stream in from miles around for a day of frenzied trading.

The Plaza de Ponchos is the epicentre of the crafts melee, a blazing labyrinth of makeshift passageways endless ranks of tapestries, jumpers, hammocks, cloths and shawls, amid which Otavaleños dressed in all their finery lurk at strategic points to tempt potential customers. But hard sell isn't their style; gentle, good-natured coaxing is far more effective at weakening the customer's resolve. Even the most hardened skinflints will soon be stuffing their bags with everything they never knew they needed and plenty else besides. The only tricky part is deciding who back home should get the six-foot rain-stick and who gets the sheepskin chaps.

need to know

Otavalo is 86km northeast of Quito, from where there are buses every ten minutes (2hr journey). The Plaza de Ponchos market is open every day, but it's at its most impressive on Saturdays. The animal market on the western outskirts of town begins on Saturdays before dawn and winds up around 10am.

Skip the beach this year, embrace winter in July and get a tan on the sunny slopes of the Andes in the middle of Argentina's Lake District at Bariloche, a laconic town turned major South American skiing destination. Surrounded by spectacular forests, pristine rivers and lakes, rifted valleys and towering alpine peaks and with average seasonal temperatures around 4°C (40°F), it's no wonder that this is prime ski country for South Americans. Luckily, since the rest of the world hasn't quite caught on, you won't spend a fortune on rentals and lift tickets, or wait a lifetime in line.

Start by hitting the slopes at Cerro Catedral, the oldest, largest and most developed ski resort in South America, featuring a new gondola, a vertical drop of 1070m and over 75km of marked trails, gullies and chutes – the longest run is 4km long – to say nothing of the off-piste possibilities, with back-country riding that rivals anything in the French Alps or Colorado. Skiing is a lot less common in South America than elsewhere in the world, and mid-level skiers will find themselves in plenty of good company here. On the other hand, if you're a superstar on the snow, the more challenging pistes are much less crowded and yours for the shredding.

Unlike the massive resorts of US and European ski centres, Argentina's mountain destinations are decidedly more low-key in terms of their sprawl, though don't think for a moment that this means there is less going on. Argentines are well known for their indulgence in the refined institution of après-ski, and Bariloche's off-slope adventures include dozens of discos, casinos and wine bars, with ample restaurants for savouring Argentina's scrumptious cuisine. After all, what would a week (a month? an entire season?) on the slopes be without exploring the excellent winter nightlife?

Bariloche is located an hour's flight from Buenos Aires; several flights ply the route daily. **Cerro Catedral** (@www.catedralaltapatagonia.com) has lift tickets from US$20–40, depending on the dates. Ski season lasts from late May until early October, with the peak season running from mid-July to early August.

Going 14
downhill
in the Andes

15

Rafting on **sacred waters** in Urubamba Valley

Snaking along from the Andes out to the Apurímac in the Amazon basin, the mighty Urubamba is the main fluvial artery pulsing through the Incas' heartland, winding between many of their most revered sites, making the river itself sacred. Not all the Urubamba is negotiable by craft, but one section, not far from the start of the Inca Trail, is perfect for a bit of gentle whitewater rafting.

On the first stretch, a serene meander through the Urubamba Valley, novice rafters will have the chance to get used to the feeling of having nothing but inflated plastic between them and some fairly sharp rocks. This is a chance to enjoy the superb views of the snowy peaks of the Andes in the distance on one side, and the wooded slopes of the valley stretching up hundreds of metres on the other, where Quechua-speaking llama herders ply the steep trails of their ancestors and the distinctive black and white forms of condors can be seen wheeling far above. Blink and you'll miss the rows of ancient Inca grain stores, carved from rock and piled impossibly high on the emerald green banks.

Don't be lulled into thinking this is naught but a pleasure boat. The roar of the rapids quickly gets louder as the raft moves faster. Following the instructor's command, you'll row harder and duck lower as the raft shoots down increasingly larger and faster falls. However secular you are, you may find yourself praying to the ancient spirits of the Incas as you go rushing down the final and biggest drop along this beginner's stretch. There are scarier, more dangerous river rapids in Peru for experienced rafters – the excellent class V rapids of the Colca Canyon, for instance. But none can rival the beauty and majesty of the sacred river of the Incas.

need to know

Rafting trips can easily be arranged in Cusco. The rapids on the Urubamba are Class III and suitable for beginners, but make sure the rafting outfit has decent equipment – lifejackets and helmets are essential, while wetsuits are a nice touch, as spills into the icy water are common – and the instructions are clear.

Getting swept off
your feet in

Buenos Aires

*W*hen it first emerged in the city's brothels and slums sometime in the 1890s, the world's sexiest ballroom dance, the tango, horrified the genteel classes of Buenos Aires. But some of the more liberal-minded upper-class youths fell in love with tango and brought it to Paris, where the dance's characteristic haunting melodies, seductive gazes and prostitute-inspired split skirts took the capital of passion by storm. By the 1910s tango's popularity had gone global, but Buenos Aires was and remains the spiritual and professional home of both the music form and dance.

If you want to keep a low profile, head to a tango show – aimed squarely at tourists, these are glitzy, polished, expensive affairs where the dance is performed on stage by professionals. More earthy and authentic – and worth seeking out – are the *milongas*, or tango gatherings, where everyone takes part. These range from stately mid-afternoon affairs in the city's exquisite Art Deco tea salons to smoky, late-night events behind unmarked doors deep in the suburbs, and to youthful tango-meets-techno *milongas* in the city's trendy districts.

It's perfectly acceptable to turn up, albeit smartly dressed, and simply enjoy the music while watching the dancers glide with apparent ease across the floor. But beware: the music and the locals may have you under their spell – and in their arms – faster than you may have anticipated.

need to know

Venues and times of *milongas* are forever changing, so you will need to seek local advice when you arrive. A good place to start is Ⓦwww.tangodata.com.ar, run by the city government, which has weekly listings. Long-running *milongas* include the traditional Tango Ideal at the **Confitería Ideal** Suipacha 384, and the hip Parakultural events in Palermo (Ⓦwww. parakultural.com.ar). Some *milongas* are preceded by a tango lesson, though you'll need several of these – and, if you're a woman, a pair of killer heels – before you can master the basics of this fairly complex dance.

17

Punta del Este

The continent's most exclusive beach resort by far, Punta del Este is Uruguay's answer to Saint Tropez. There's a certain level of celebrity that's achieved simply by being here. If you don that outrageously expensive Sauvage swimsuit, act like you belong and hit the beach, chances are you may end up in the pages of a South American glossy mag. Punta is largely about glitzy casinos, all-night parties, designer sushi and fashionistas sipping frozen mojitos. It's the kind of place where you might spot Naomi Campbell and Prince Albert of Monaco on the same evening – though probably not in the same Ferrari convertible. Every January half a million visitors – mostly Argentines and Brazilians – cram themselves in between surfers' paradise Playa Brava and family-friendly Playa Mansa, so you can easily lose yourself in the crowds.

need to know

Punta del Este's Laguna del Sauce airport is only 30 minutes from Buenos Aires' Aeroparque Jorge Newbery domestic aerodrome (national carriers Pluna and Aerolíneas Argentinas both fly there, 10–16 flights daily). The high season is January and February – making November and March ideal for avoiding crowds.

But there's another side to Punta. Leave the Quiksilver-clad funboarders and world beach-volley tournaments behind and head for one of the infinite golden *playas* way beyond Punta Ballena, on the River Plate side of things. Explore Chihuahua where you can sunbathe among the enormous straw-hued dunes, take cover in the secluded pine groves and even venture into the tepid waters. At night, drive across the landmark rollercoaster bridge to La Barra – ignore the bronzed beauties queuing for flambéed lobster along the main drag – and race past the windswept ocean strands to José Ignacio. Dine in discreet style right on the seafront. Enjoy your simply barbecued squid and chilled sauvignon blanc, listen to the breakers crashing onto the sand, feel the Atlantic breeze in your hair. And rest assured that the shutterbugs are all busy snapping the heir to the Spanish throne at some heaving cocktail bar in Punta.

18 WATCHING A FOOTBALL MATCH

Few sporting events rival the raucous spectacle of a football match in South America. From a small, local but enthusiastically supported game in the Andes to a clash of the titans in one of the great cathedrals of the sport in Brazil or Argentina, even those who can't tell a goal kick from a penalty kick won't fail to be impressed by the colour and passion – both on the pitch and in the stands.

Fans of the sport can look forward to fast, attacking football, individual star turns, lots of goals (0-0 draws are practically unheard of, as is defensive play), red cards aplenty and quite possibly a pitch invasion.

The bigger the team, the bigger the stadium, and the louder the roar of the crowd. Choose Rio's Maracanã, one the world's largest, São Paulo's Art Deco Pacaembú, or Buenos Aires' Bombonera ("chocolate box", for its shape) for a full-on assault of the senses – particularly if you time your visit for a local derby such as São Paulo v Corinthians or Boca Juniors v River Plate.

As well as their teams' jersey, fans will go armed with ticker tape, flags, flares, horns and drums. Don't be surprised if you can hardly see the players through the resulting clouds of red, blue or yellow. You certainly won't be able to miss the supporters' loud and, ahem, colourful singing before, during and after the match, whether their team wins or loses, accompanied by entire brass bands and battalions of drummers. After a big game, follow the (winning) crowds to the boisterous after-match street parties.

NEED TO KNOW

The Brazilian and Argentine football year is split into two seasons (late July to early December and late January to early June), though the summer and winter recesses are also sprinkled with mini-tournaments and international fixtures. Tickets are normally available from the ground on match day, although for some of the big clashes you may need to buy several days ahead; travel agents in the big cities can sort tickets and transport. The frenetic all-standing terraces (*popular* in Argentina, *geral* in Brazil) are the cheapest (and noisiest) part of the stands, but first-time attendees are advised to head to the relative calm of the seating area (*platea* or *arquibancada* respectively).

Set against the parched grasslands of the Altiplano, the deep, sapphire blue waters of the world's highest navigable lake, Lago Titicaca, offer the promise of life and fertility in this arid region, where all agriculture is dependent on irrigation or capricious rainfall. The Incas believed the creator god Viracocha rose from the waters of this lake, calling forth the sun and the moon to light up the world, from an island in its centre now called the Isla del Sol – the Island of the Sun.

Claiming their own dynasty also originated there, they built a complex of shrines and temples on the island, transforming it into a religious centre of enormous importance, a pan-Andean pilgrimage destination once visited by thousands of worshippers annually from across their vast empire.

Modern visitors can follow the same route as the pilgrims of Inca times, travelling by boat from the port town of Copacabana – itself a pilgrimage centre for the now nominally-Christian population of the Bolivian highlands.

With no roads or cars on the island, the only way to visit the Inca ruins is on foot, trekking through the tranquil villages of the indigenous Aymara who raise crops on the intricate agricultural terraces left by the Incas, and who still regard Lago Titicaca as a powerful female deity capable of regulating climate and rainfall.

The ruined temples themselves are small in comparison to Inca sites elsewhere in the Andes, but the setting more than makes up for this. The great rock where the sun and moon were created looks out on all sides across the tranquil expanse of the lake, which is in turn surrounded by mighty snowcapped mountains, each of which is still worshipped as a deity in its own right. The serene beauty of this sacred Andean geography imparts a powerful spiritual energy, which makes it easy to believe this could indeed be the centre of the universe.

19

Making a pilgrimage to the

Isla del Sol

need to know Boats to the Isla del Sol depart every morning from the lakeside pilgrimage town of Copacabana. It's easy to arrange to be dropped off at one end of the island and picked up at the other at the end of the day, leaving time to walk between the various Inca sites. Copacabana is a 3–4hr bus journey from Bolivia's main city, La Paz, and is also easy to reach from the city of Puno, just across the border in Peru.

From the vantage point of a Cessna, the great expanse of Guyana's rainforest interior looks like billows of green cloud. A little plane drones over the soft canopy, low enough that the passengers can almost blow and the trees would disperse like smoke, revealing whatever mysteries lie hidden beneath. About an hour out of Georgetown, just as the unbroken jungle scenery starts to get monotonous, the plane banks sharply to the right, losing roughly half of its altitude in a couple of seconds, and heads down towards a gorge bordered by thick forest. As the plane descends farther, a waterfall soon comes into view, cascading down the middle of the gorge, not in tumultuous rumbles of white foam, but in a single rapier-like gush of water that seems to come from nowhere and disappear into nowhere.

Enjoying the kind of splendid isolation that Niagara Falls can only dream of, Kaieteur Falls is five times as high as Niagara and infinitely more enigmatic. The narrow band of water that runs off the side of the Kaieteur Gorge plunges 226m to the bottom, making the falls here the highest single-drop waterfall in the world. Flying close enough to hear the water's roar blend menacingly with the sound of whirring propellers, it all seems dark and forbidding down below. The plane's passengers may start to worry about those hardy souls who opted to walk through the rainforest for several days in order to reach the falls, getting their first glimpse of Kaieteur dropping on top of them – a somewhat intimidating experience when compared with the exhilaration of flying in, but no less awesome.

need to know Day-trips by plane to Kaieteur Falls from Georgetown cost US$230 from **Wilderness Explorers** (⊛www .wilderness-explorers.com) and include a visit to Orinduik Falls on the Brazilian border, where you can go swimming. Kaieteur Falls is at its widest and most dramatic during Guyana's wet season (April–August).

20

Kaieteur Falls

21

Catching a launch at the Centre Spatial Guyanais

Completed in 1968, the Centre Spatial Guyanais (CSG) is something straight out of a James Bond movie. Rocket launch towers, futuristic silos and other state-of-the-art technology poke out above the trees in the rainforest surrounding Kourou. Once a quiet, nondescript village in the French overseas *département* – and former penal colony – of Guyane (French Guiana), it was discovered that Kourou was the only place in the world where both polar and equatorial synchronous orbits could be achieved. Almost overnight, French Guiana was transformed from a Hell-on-Earth for France's hapless convicts (the penal colony was abolished in 1947) to the epicentre of the European Space Agency's satellite-launching operations.

Nowadays Kourou is bustling with technicians in jump-suits scurrying about with clipboards in hand, and occasionally the French Foreign Legion patrols the perimeters, protecting the CSG from spies and other such threats. This isolated, surreal and, it must be said, slightly sinister space centre in the jungle outdoes anything that NASA's Florida-based Kennedy Space Center has to offer, at least as far as sci-fi-fantasy-meets-reality is concerned. "Ariane" 5 rockets have been blasting off from the CSG since 1996, carrying payloads consisting mainly of satellites. Launches take place in the early evening, just after the sun has set and the enigmatic, nocturnal sounds of the rainforest draw attention to the eerie coexistence of extreme technology and extreme nature. Hundreds, sometimes thousands, of people gather to watch the take-off. With an almighty roar, the rocket lifts into the sky, leaving a great plume of white smoke and a blinding sheet of fire in its wake that lights up the trees and warms the faces of the starry-eyed onlookers.

need to know

Launches at the Centre Spatial Guyanais take place roughly every two months. If you want to watch the launch from the closer observation sites (7.5km from the launch site), you have to request an invitation by writing to: **CNES-Centre Spatial Guyanais**, Service Communication, BP 726, 97387 Kourou Cedex. Another observation site, 15km from the launch site, is free for everyone to use without invitation. For information on launch dates, visit ⓦwww.cnes-csg.fr.

Often referred to as the "Serengeti of the Americas", Los Llanos stretches infinitely from the foothills of the Andes to the lowlands of the Orinoco Delta, covering 240,000 square miles, roughly one third of Venezuela. Given that this soggy jungle (with an annual rainfall that would make Northwest England seem Saharan) is home to some pretty sinister and gigantic snakes, rodents and flesh-eating fish, it's not surprising that the intense, raw nature of Los Llanos isn't every tour guide's recommended taste of Venezuela. However, with its spectacular stock of birds, reptiles, and mammals, it justifiably ranks as one of Latin America's premier wildlife spotting destinations, and an epic setting in which to experience the traditions of the Llanero cowboy, the region's stoical protagonist who embodies the independent spirit of this country that still adheres to ancient traditions.

22 Walk on the *wild side* in Los Llanos

The ultimate way to unleash your inner jungle cowboy is to stay as a guest at Hato El Cedral, a 130,000-acre working cattle ranch renowned for its conservation projects. It doesn't take long to get into lasso-whirling character here and you can forget the cocktails with umbrellas and chic cuisine and get used to the ranch's sturdy all-beef menu, unless of course you fancy trying your luck at piranha fishing – a local delicacy in a region where nothing is wasted. When the cowboys aren't driving the region's 12 million cattle huge distances across the plains, guests are treated to their lonesome and often spine-curdling stories. Or better yet, you may catch the Llaneros competing in verbal jousts, known as *contrapunteo* - improvised verses with themes about anything from a forsaken damsel, to an adipose capybara, to the general woes of life on the plains.

need to know

Wildlife spotting opportunities are dramatically improved during the dry Season (November to May) when animals gather around sparse water sources. **Hato El Cedral** (ⓦwww.hatocedral.com) is a nine-hour drive from Caracas or a one-and-a-half hour charter to Aeropuerto de Mantecal, a thirty-minute journey by car from El Cedral. Double rooms cost between US$100 and US$120 per person, per night. Safari-style land and water excursions are offered twice daily.

Following ancient
FOOTSTEPS
on the INCA TRAIL

Once the stomping ground for colourfully dressed Incas paying homage to the mountain gods, after five hundred years the Inca Trail still wends its way between towering glaciated peaks, and local Indians still follow the same route, albeit these days carrying tents and food for tourists.

Leaving the Cusco train at km88, where the trail begins, hikers make first contact with their porters. Underpaid and barefoot (or in recycled tyre sandals), these are the trek's true heroes. With their help, you don't have to be marathon-fit to climb the Inca Trail, and once you conquer its most difficult stretch, Dead Woman's Pass (Abra de Huarmihuañusca) on the second morning, the next few days are relatively easy.

Slow and steady is the best strategy for tackling the steep gradients, ancient stone steps and tunnels carved through sheer rock; along the way you'll be able to glimpse the remains of several finely built Incan palaces and temples that punctuate the trail. Even though you'll be travelling and camping with a lot of other hikers in an organized group, it's still possible to wander alone at times and soak up the stunning landscape.

Seeking sunrise at Machu Picchu, most people set off from Wiñay Wayna (the last campsite) for the final leg around 4am. After two hours through languid cloud forest the trail finishes at Intipunku, the magnificent stone entrance to Machu Picchu. This impressive gateway offers the first views across one of the greatest wonders of the world – a magical citadel of vast proportions, surrounded by impossibly precipitous terraces and perched high up above the Urubamba Valley.

need to know

You can only hike the Inca Trail as part of an organized tour group. Tours need to be booked at least six months in advance (costs from around US$300; entry to Machu Picchu is US$40). Before climbing, make sure you have acclimatized to the altitude, allowing at least three days in Cusco if you've flown straight from sea level.

In the northern half of Chile, the driest place on Earth, clouds are virtually unknown and the southern skies are of the brightest blue. At night, far away from the lights of major settlements, you can look up at a dark vault simply shimmering with stars. The near-perfect visibility almost every night of the year makes the region ideal for observing the universe – indeed, there are more astronomical observatories here than anywhere else on Earth – but you don't need to be an astronomer to get a great view.

Some of the world's most powerful computerized telescopes reside here, but you can also catch sight of constellations like the Southern Cross and familiar heavenly bodies like Jupiter or Mars at more modest observatories, such as Mamalluca. Set aside one evening, resist that extra pisco sour – the national drink made from the sugary grapes grown throughout the region – and book one of the regular stargazing tours departing in the wee hours. These take you high up on Cerro Mamalluca, where the darkness is absolute and the air is crisp. There's the classic visit – a short talk giving you a grounding in basic astronomy, followed by a few minutes looking through a telescope – or the Andean Cosmovision tour in which guides explain how the Pre-Colombian peoples interpreted the night sky, and perform native songs, with flutes and drums accompanying mystic verses, speaking of a local cosmology dating back thousands of years.

24

STARGAZING ON
Cerro Mamalluca

need to know

The nearest cities with airports to the observatories are La Serena and Antofagasta. The **European Southern Observatory (ESO)** has two sets of impressive, cutting-edge installations at La Silla and Paranal (Ⓦwww.eso.org), while the **Carnegie Institute** has space-watching facilities at Las Campañas. These observatories are all open for visits, but access to the telescopes themselves is reserved for leading astronomers. For a more hands-on experience, head for the municipal installations at Mamalluca (Ⓦwww.mamalluca.org), easily accessible from Vicuña.

A noisy concrete forest of tower blocks and brightly lit malls, Manaus throngs with shoppers braving the hot, humid streets to buy cheap electronic goods in this remote Amazonian capital and duty free zone. Glittering in the twilight and visible above the chaos and heat of downtown is a large dome whose 36,000 ceramic tiles are painted gold, green and blue, the colours of the Brazilian flag. The palatial building it presides over is a grand pink and white confection of Belle Epoque architecture, the Teatro Amazonas.

Nothing could seem more out of place. Built in the late nineteenth century during the height of Brazil's rubber boom, the lavish opera house was designed by Italians to look Parisian (indeed, almost all the materials were brought over from Europe). Abandoned for many years when the rubber industry died and Manaus could scarcely afford its electricity bill, the theatre is now funded by a large state budget and hosts regular performances of jazz and ballet, though nothing is quite so singular as its staging of top-quality opera in the middle of the jungle.

The surreal experience begins the moment you enter the foyer and step onto a floor covered in gleaming hardwood; walls are lined with columns made from the finest Carrara marble and ornate Italian frescoes decorate the ceiling. Hundreds of chandeliers hang in falling crystal formations. It's like you've been transported to a European capital, with a twist. You're ushered through red velvet curtains by men dressed in tailcoats and top hats. The orchestra, the Amazonas Philharmonic, pick up their instruments that have been specially treated to cope with the humidity of the jungle. The chatter dissipates abruptly. The conductor raises his baton, and the first familiar notes of Wagner's *Ring Cycle* fill the auditorium, then seep out languidly into the steamy night.

need to know

Manaus is accessible by plane or boat only. The Teatro Amazonas, which hosts an annual opera festival at the end of April, can be visited on a guided tour (Mon–Sat 9am–8pm, though not within two hours of a performance; US$5).

Ultimate
experiences
South
America
miscellany

 The body beautiful

The women of Brazil and Argentina are justly famous for their beauty. But for many of them, those good looks come at a great price in blood and money. Argentina and Brazil have the highest rates of **cosmetic surgery** in the world, as thousands of women turn to nose jobs, face-lifts and silicone implants in their obsessive quest for the perfect body. Elsewhere on the continent, Colombia is catching up fast, as women there turn to surgery in the hopes of landing a man who will take them out of poverty, a phenomenon captured perfectly in the hugely popular television soap opera, *Sin tetas no hay paraíso* – "Without (big) breasts, there is no paradise".

 Birdwatching

South America's immense biodiversity makes it a birdwatcher's paradise; it's home to more than 3000 species of bird – a third of the global total – from tiny hummingbirds and exuberant macaws to the mighty condor and giant flightless rhea. Some individual national parks, such as Manu in southern Peru, support more bird species than the whole of North America.

Coffee

The plant may have originated in Africa, but South America has a strong claim to producing the best coffee in the world. The largest producers, Brazil and Colombia, are also the most passionate consumers, and both tend to keep the best of their coffee crop to themselves. In Colombia, mild black coffee known as *tinto* is sold on every street corner, while in Brazil, small, strong cups of *cafezinho* are seen as an essential accompaniment to almost every activity.

 # Coca

Demonized in Europe and the United States as the raw material for the production of cocaine, the small green coca leaf has been used for thousands of years by the indigenous people of the Andes as both a mild stimulant and a key ingredient in traditional rituals and medicine. In Peru and Bolivia, where it's still legal, it's considered an important symbol of indigenous identity. When made into an herbal tea, it's also a useful treatment for altitude sickness.

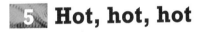 # Hot, hot, hot

Native to South America, hot chilli peppers and the countless sauces they can be turned into are the main condiment almost everywhere you go in the region. As well as enlivening sometimes bland or repetitive food, they offer a powerful defence against stomach bugs and parasites. Proceed with caution, though, as some varieties – such as *rocoto* in Peru – possess extraordinary strength, bringing tears to the eyes of even experienced chilli-eaters.

 # El Dorado

Machu Picchu in Peru is the most famous of the many cities built by indigenous civilizations in South America that fell into ruin and were lost after the Spanish conquest. Despite centuries of exploration, legends persist of fabulous cities of gold known as Paititi or El Dorado, hidden deep in the Amazon rainforest or the remote Andes and indeed substantial new ruins are still discovered every few years.

▶▶ Five lost cities

Ciudad Perdida. Hidden in the Sierra Nevada de Santa Marta, Colombia
Vilcabamba. The last refuge of the Incas in the forest-covered foothills of the southern Peruvian Andes.
Kuelap. Massive stone citadel of the Chachapoyas culture in northern Peru.
Choquequirau. Long-forgotten Inca citadel in southern Peru.
Gran Pajaten Sprawling urban complex controversially "rediscovered" in the cloud forests of northern Peru.

7 Five great movies on South America

Blood of the Condor (Yawar Mallku), 1968. Scathing attack on the impact of US imperialism on the indigenous people of the Bolivian Andes.

Central Station, 1998. Heart-rending story of a Brazilian woman who abandons her cynicism to help a homeless boy search for the father he's never known.

City of God, 2002. Gripping portrayal of life and death among the teenage drug gangs in the slums of Rio de Janeiro.

The Motorcycle Diaries, 2004. Delightful adaptation of Che Guevara's diary, in which the future revolutionary and a friend travel across South America by motorbike in search of adventure.

The Official Story, 1985. Harrowing tale of an Argentine woman who has to face the truth about military rule as she discovers her adopted daughter (one of the "disappeared") was stolen from her.

8 Fiestas

South Americans welcome any excuse for a party, and across the region the annual calendar is punctuated with anniversaries, public holidays and local saint's days on which eating, drinking and making merry is pretty much obligatory, and work impossible. Some of these fiestas last a week or more. These are some of the most famous and universal.

Virgen de la Candelaria (2 February). Saint's Day of a particular representation of the Virgin Mary revered in many South American cities including Puno in Peru and Copacabana in Bolivia, where the fiesta is marked by multitudinous folkloric parades.

Carnaval (late February or early March). The pre-Lenten carnival celebrated all over South America. The most famous and extravagant is of course in Rio, but other cities such as Salvador da Bahia in Brazil, Oruro in Bolivia, and Baranquilla in Colombia also hold massive and extraordinary celebrations.

Semana Santa (March or April). The Easter Holy Week is marked throughout the region with colourful religious processions. The most fervent and dramatic are in Ayacucho in Peru, Mérida in Venezuela and Popayán in Colombia.

Corpus Christi (June). Another major Catholic religious festival celebrated with processions and costumed dancers, most notably in Peru and Venezuela.

Todos Santos/Dia de los Muertos (November 1 & 2). On all Saint's Day people in Peru and Bolivia go to the cemetery to commemorate their dead relatives, bringing them food and drink and sometimes taking them out of their tombs.

 Food

With its mixture of European, African, Asian and indigenous influences, not to mention the ready availability of almost every possible agricultural product, South America boasts some fantastic food, and the portions are invariably generous. The finest national cuisines are considered to be those of Peru, Argentina and Brazil, in that order.

▸▸ Five dishes not to miss

Argentine beef Quite simply, these are the finest steaks and roasts in the world.

Ceviche A cool yet spicy Peruvian dish of raw fish and seafood marinated in lime juice and hot chilli, best served with an ice-cold beer.

Cuy Guinea pigs are the oldest domesticated animal in the Americas and still considered a treat by the indigenous Andean people of Peru and Ecuador. Roasted on a spit, they have a delicious, gamey taste, once you get past the fact you're eating a rodent.

Feijoada Classic Brazilian stew of black beans, meat and sausages.

Hormiga culona Big-butt queen ants are a prized delicacy in northern Colombia, with a nutty, almost chocolate-like flavour.

10 Football

It's often said that the unofficial religion of South America is **football** (*futbol* in Spanish, *futebol* in Portuguese). Everywhere you go in the continent you'll find people watching, talking about and playing what's known as the beautiful game. Almost every village has a football pitch, even if it's the only flat piece of land in an Andean community, and it's not unusual to come across South Americans who are the proud owners of a pair of football boots but have no other shoes. The immense skill and flamboyant creativity of South American football has captured the imagination of the world, with Uruguay, Argentina and Brazil producing a series of World Cup-winning teams. The continent has also produced the two greatest footballers the world has ever seen: Argentine Diego Maradona and Brazilian Edson Arantes do Nascimiento, better known as Pelé.

11 Hammocks

Of all the inventions of the indigenous peoples of South America, the hammock is surely the greatest contribution to world civilization. Strung up in an instant anywhere there are trees, roof beams or upright poles, the hammock is both a perfect place to adjust to the local pace of life and a cool and comfortable alternative to a bed.

12 Five unforgettable hotels

Alvear Palace Hotel, Buenos Aires, Argentina. Exquisite 1930s hotel in the heart of the Argentine capital, oozing with class and old world charm

Albergue Ecológico Chalalán, Parque Nacional Madidi, Bolivia. Traditionally built eco-lodge run by the indigenous Quechua-Tacana people in the heart of the Amazon rainforest.

Hacienda Los Lingues, San Fernando, Chile. Beautifully preserved colonial hacienda converted into a luxury hotel but still inhabited and operated as a ranch by one of Chile's most aristocratic families.

Hotel Glória, Rio de Janeiro, Brazil. A palatial 1920s luxury hotel with an unrivalled setting close to the centre of Rio, offering spectacular views of the city.

Hotel Monasterio, Cusco, Peru. Luxurious establishment set in a beautifully restored sixteenth century Spanish colonial monastery.

 # Language

South America is dominated by two main languages brought over by European conquerors in the sixteenth century: **Portuguese** in Brazil, and **Spanish** almost everywhere else. The exceptions are the small countries of Guyana, French Guiana (technically part of France) and Surinam, which are English, French and Dutch-speaking respectively. Throughout the continent, hundreds of indigenous languages that existed before the conquest are still spoken, some by only a few hundred people, others by nations of millions. These are particularly concentrated in the Andean regions of Peru, Bolivia and Ecuador and in Paraguay, which has the highest level of bilingualism in the world.

▶▶ Main indigenous languages

Quechua	Peru, Bolivia, Ecuador, Colombia, Argentina
Guaraní	Paraguay, Argentina, Bolivia, Brazil
Aymara	Bolivia, Peru, Chile, Argentina
Mapudungun (Mapuche)	Chile, Argentina
Wayuu	Colombia, Venezuela

"God is big, but the forest is bigger."
Brazilian proverb

 **Liberators**

In most South American countries the wars of independence from Spain in the early nineteenth century are seen as national epics of sacrifice and heroism, and the leaders of those struggles are lionized as near-godlike figures. None is more revered than Simón Bolívar, known as the Liberator, whose armies drove the Spanish out of Venezuela, Colombia, Ecuador, Peru and finally Bolivia, which was named in his honour. You'll find statues of Bolívar throughout South America, above all in his native Venezuela, where any disrespect to his image can still get you in serious trouble.

Many South Americans accord similar reverence to the Argentine communist guerrilla Ernesto "Che" Guevara whose death in Bolivia in 1967 while trying to launch a continent-wide revolution inspired a generation of left-wingers to take up arms against the state, usually with disastrous consequences.

"Those who serve a revolution plough the sea."

Simón Bolívar

 **Literature**

South American writers burst onto the world literary scene in the 1960s with the arrival of magical realism, a style that captures the romance and allure of the continent. Many of the best writers are well translated, but if you're learning Spanish or Portuguese it's well worth having a go at the original texts.

▶▶ **Classic South American literature**

Of Love and Shadows by Isabel Allende. Powerful love story set in an imaginary country of arbitrary arrests, sudden disappearances and summary executions that closely resembles the author's Chilean homeland in the 1970s and '80s.

Dona Flor and Her Two Husbands by Jorge Amado. Supernatural romance set in the Brazilian state of Bahia. When Flor's first husband comes back from the dead, how can she resist his advances?

Labyrinths by Jorge Luis Borges. Collection of essays and short stories that encapsulate the unique style and approach of Argentina's greatest writer.

One Hundred Years of Solitude by Gabriel García Marquéz. Epic tale of a Colombian family in love and war that defined the magical realist style of fiction.

Conversation in the Cathedral by Mario Vargas Llosa. A labyrinth of power, corruption and the search for identity in Peru.

▶▶ Books on South America

In Patagonia by Bruce Chatwin. Beautifully written account of a trip to the far south of the continent whose spare prose style and imaginative approach inspired a new generation of travel writers.

Conquest of the Incas by John Hemming. Definitive account of how a handful of desperate Spanish adventurers conquered the greatest indigenous empire in South America.

Tristes Tropiques by Claude Lévi-Strauss. Fascinating work by the legendary French anthropologist studying indigenous cultures in Brazil in the 1930s.

The Fruit Palace by Charles Nichol. Hilarious and frightening investigation of the cocaine business in Colombia.

Marching Powder by Rusty Young. Surreal and terrifying description of the experiences of an Englishman's life in Bolivia's most notorious prison.

"The problem with marriage is that it ends every night after making love, and it must be rebuilt every morning before breakfast."

Gabriel García Marquéz

16 Machismo

As far as much of its male population is concerned, South America remains a land where men are men and women are subservient. The cultural stereotype of machismo – which characterizes men as strong and dominant and women as weak and submissive – is alive and well, although it's facing a growing feminist challenge. Women are widely viewed as either virgins or whores, and outside the main cities, attitudes toward homosexuality are similarly unreconstructed.

17 Mañana, mañana

South Americans have a very different attitude toward time and punctuality than people from other cultures. Arriving hours or even days late for a meeting barely warrants an explanation, never mind an apology, and almost anything that can be put off until tomorrow (*mañana*), will be.

18 Mountains

Running the length of South America like a spine from the Caribbean coast to the far southern tip of Patagonia, the Andes form the longest and second-highest mountain chain in the world. All the highest peaks are in the far south of the continent along the border between Chile and Argentina, but the highest inhabited areas are in the tropical latitudes of Peru, Ecuador and Bolivia, where entire cities exist at up to 4000 metres above sea level.

▶▶ Highest Andean peaks

Aconcagua	6959m	Argentina
Ojos del Salado	6893m	Chile (world's highest volcano)
Monte Pissis	6795m	Argentina
Bonete	6759m	Argentina
Tres Cruces Sur	6748m	Argentina/Chile

 19 Music and dance

South Americans abhor silence, and wherever you go you'll be surrounded by music that encapsulates the majesty of the landscape and the idiosyncrasy of the people, from the haunting panpipes of the high Andes, to the African rhythms of Brazil and the Caribbean and the sensuous urban decadence of the tango.

▶▶ Five ways to dance the night away

Salsa in Cali, Colombia.
Tango in Buenos Aires, Argentina.
Samba in Rio de Janeiro, Brazil.
Huayno in Cusco, Peru.
Merengue in Caracas, Venezuela.

20 Natural attractions

Galápagos Islands, Ecuador. Extraordinary archipelago whose unique population of land and marine wildlife inspired Charles Darwin's theory of evolution.

Iguazú Falls, Brazil and Argentina. Massive and stunningly beautiful collection of nearly three hundred waterfalls that plunge over a precipice 80m high and 3km wide.

Manu Biosphere Reserve, southern Peru. Encompassing probably the best-preserved stretch of Amazon rainforest anywhere in the region as well as high Andean peaks.

The Pantanal, Brazil. The world's biggest wetland or freshwater swamp, home to an astonishing array of wildlife.

Torres del Paine National Park, Chilean Patagonia. Mountain range of spectacular near-vertical pinnacles of granite surrounded by a pristine wilderness of glaciers, lakes and forests.

 # **People**

South America has a **population** of extraordinary diversity, drawn from all continents of the world, the legacy of its colonial history. To varying degrees every country is home to a mix of people descended from European colonists and settlers, the African slaves they brought with them and the original indigenous population. There are also sizeable Asian communities throughout the continent. While many people identify themselves as black, white or indigenous, many more are of mixed race. Ethnicity remains a powerful dividing line in most countries, with white people more likely to be in positions of wealth and power, and black and indigenous people much more likely to be poor. The largest indigenous populations are found in the Andean countries of Ecuador, Bolivia and Peru, while Argentina and Chile are seen as the most European.

 # **Politics**

After decades of often brutal military dictatorship in the twentieth century, all South American countries are now democracies, however imperfect or corrupt. However, the memory of military rule runs deep, particularly in countries (such as Chile and Argentina) that suffered so-called "dirty wars" in which thousands of people were tortured and murdered by the armed forces, or else "disappeared". Many of the killers were protected by amnesties passed as a condition for a return to civilian government, but these are now under attack as the victims and their families press for truth and justice.

 # **Rivers**

▶▶ **South America's three great rivers**

Amazon	Peru, Colombia, Brazil	6387km
La Plata	Paraguay and Argentina	3998km
Orinoco	Colombia and Venezuela	2410km

 **Religion**

The vast majority of people in South America are Roman Catholics, following the religion brought over by the Spanish and Portuguese conquerors in the sixteenth century. However, many combine their Catholicism with animist religious beliefs inherited from their indigenous ancestors, often involving the worship of natural features such as mountains and rivers. African beliefs brought over by slaves in the colonial period also remain strong in regions with large black populations, particularly Brazil. And recent decades have also seen a surge in the number of people turning to Evangelical Protestant sects, many of them funded from the United States.

Five choice souvenirs

Hammocks from Colombia.

Panama hats from Ecuador (despite the name, that's where they come from.)

Ponchos and other weavings from the indigenous markets of the Andes.

Magical candomblé beads from Brazil.

Yerba Maté cups and drinking straws from Argentina.

Ultimate experiences South America small print

South America
The complete experience

ROUGH GUIDES – don't just travel

We hope you've been inspired by the experiences in this book. To us, they sum up what makes South America such an extraordinary and stimulating place to travel. There are 24 other books in the 25 Ultimate Experiences series, each conceived to whet your appetite for travel and for everything the world has to offer. As well as covering the globe, the 25s series also includes books on **Journeys, World Food, Adventure Travel, Places to Stay, Ethical Travel, Wildlife Adventures** and **Wonders of the World**.

When you start planning your trip, Rough Guides' new-look guides, maps and phrasebooks are the ultimate companions. For 25 years we've been refining what makes a good guidebook and we now include more colour photos and more information – on average 50% more pages – than any of our competitors. Just look for the sky-blue spines.

Rough Guides don't just travel – we also believe in getting the most out of life without a passport. Since the publication of the bestselling Rough Guides to **The Internet** and **World Music**, we've brought out a wide range of lively and authoritative guides on everything from **Climate Change** to **Hip-Hop**, from **MySpace** to **Film Noir** and from **The Brain** to **The Rolling Stones**.

Publishing information

Rough Guide 25 Ultimate experiences
South America Published May 2007 by
Rough Guides Ltd, 80 Strand, London WC2R
0RL
345 Hudson St, 4th Floor,
New York, NY 10014, USA
14 Local Shopping Centre, Panchsheel Park,
New Delhi 110017, India
Distributed by the Penguin Group
Penguin Books Ltd,
80 Strand, London WC2R 0RL
Penguin Group (USA)
375 Hudson Street, NY 10014, USA
Penguin Group (Australia)
250 Camberwell Road, Camberwell,
Victoria 3124, Australia
Penguin Books Canada Ltd,
10 Alcorn Avenue, Toronto, Ontario,
Canada M4V 1E4
Penguin Group (NZ)
67 Apollo Drive, Mairangi Bay, Auckland
1310, New Zealand
Printed in China
© Rough Guides 2007

80pp
A catalogue record for this book is available
from the British Library
ISBN: 978-1-84353-826-1

The publishers and authors have done their
best to ensure the accuracy and currency
of all the information in Rough Guide 25
Ultimate experiences South America,
however, they can accept no responsibility
for any loss, injury, or inconvenience
sustained by any traveller as a result of
information or advice contained in the
guide.

1   3   5   7   9   8   6   4   2

Rough Guide credits

Editor: April Isaacs
Design & picture research: Diana Jarvis
Cartography: Katie Lloyd-Jones
Cover design: Diana Jarvis, Chloë Roberts

Production: Aimee Hampson, Katherine
Owers
Proofreader: Joseph Petta

The authors

Caroline Lascom (Experiences 1, 9, 22)
contributes to Rough Guides to Chicago
and Mexico.
Harry Adès (Experiences 2, 7, 12) is a co-
author of Rough Guides to Ecuador and
South America.
Joshua Goodman (Experience 3) is a co-
author of the Rough Guide to South America.
Andrew Benson (Experiences 4, 13, 17, 24)
is a co-author of Rough Guides to Chile,
Argentina and South America.
James Read (Experiences 5, 10, 11, 19 and
Miscellany) is the author of the Rough Guide
to Bolivia and a co-author of First-Time Latin
America.
Paul D Smith (Experience 6) writes for the
Rough Guide to South America.

Richard Danbury (Experience 8) has
contributed to the Rough Guide to Chile and
authors a guide to walking the Inca Trail.
Roger Norum (Experience 14) is a co-author
of the Rough Guide to Denmark and has
travelled extensively in Latin America.
Rosalba O'Brien (Experiences 15, 16, 18) is
a co-author of the Rough Guide to Argentina.
Ross Velton (Experience 20, 21) writes several
Rough Guides, including the Rough Guide to
South America.
Dilwyn Jenkins (Experience 23) is the author
of Rough Guides to Peru and Brazil.
Polly Rodger Brown (Experience 25) is a co-
author of First-Time Latin America.

Picture credits

Fly Less – Stay Longer!

Rough Guides believes in the good that travel does, but we are deeply aware of the impact of fuel emissions on climate change. We recommend taking fewer trips and staying for longer. If you can avoid travelling by air, please use an alternative, especially for journeys under 1000km/600miles. And always offset your travel at **www.roughguides.com/climatechange**.

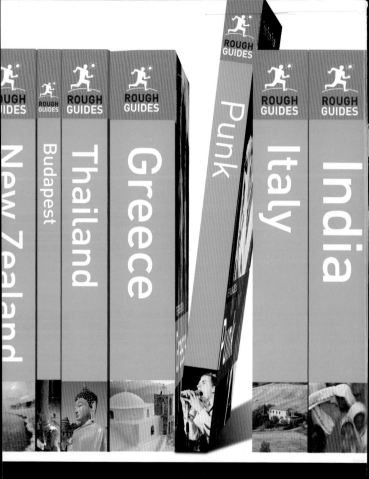

ROUGH GUIDES

ROUGH GUIDES

ROUGH GUIDES

ROUGH GUIDES

ROUGH GUIDES

ROUGH GUIDES

ROUGH GUIDES

New Zealand

Budapest

Thailand

Greece

Punk

Italy

India

Over 70 reference books and hundreds of travel
guides, maps & phrasebooks that cover the world.

ROUGH GUIDES · ROUGH GUIDES · ROUGH GUIDES · ROUGH GUIDES · ROUGH GUIDES · ROUGH GUIDES · ROUGH GUIDES

Australia

Cuba

Britain

Singapore

Vietnam

New York City

Morocco

BROADEN YOUR HORIZONS
www.roughguides.com

ROUGH GUIDES 25 YEARS

Index